Little Swin

Magdalena Dabrowska & Agnieszka Peszek

Little Swimmer

Improve Your Child's Confidence And Physical Development

Meyer & Meyer Sport

British Library Cataloguing in Publication Data
A catalogue record for this book is available from the British Library

Little Swimmer
Maidenhead: Meyer & Meyer Sport (UK) Ltd., 2014
ISBN: 978-1-78255-012-9

Original Title: Mały pływak
© 2011 by landie.pl Ltd.
Translation: landie.pl

© 2014 by Meyer & Meyer Sport (UK) Ltd.
Aachen, Auckland, Beirut, Budapest, Cairo, Cape Town, Dubai, Hägendorf, Indianapolis, Maidenhead, Singapore, Sydney, Tehran, Wien

 Member of the World Sport Publishers' Association (WSPA) www.w-s-p-a.org

Printed by: B.O.S.S Druck und Medien GmbH, Germany
ISBN: 978-1-78255-012-9
E-Mail: info@m-m-sports.com
www.m-m-sports.com

Table of Contents

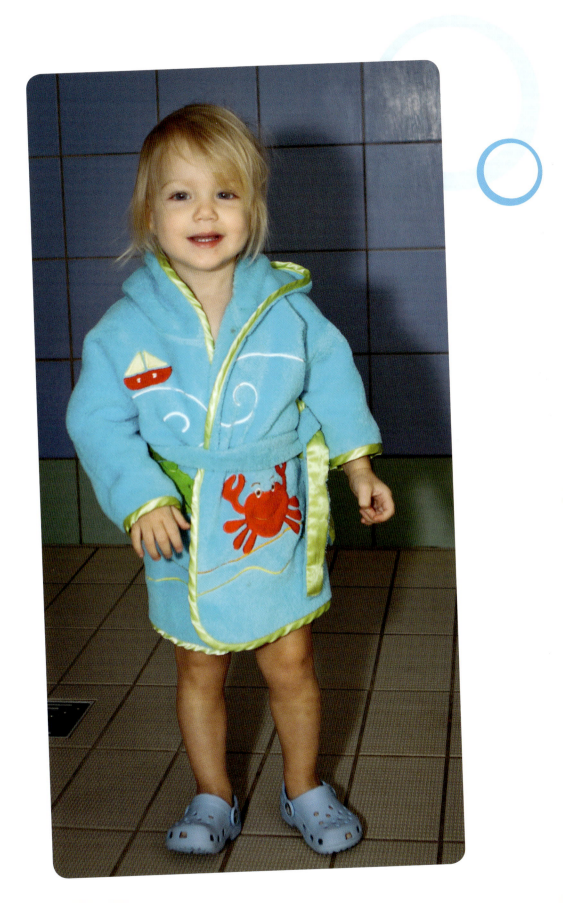

Little Heroes
(in alphabetical order)

Amelia

I am 8 months old. I have been swimming since I was 3 months old and I love it. I am also very talkative and active. When I am not asleep, I am always moving. I love to ride on my lion.

Julka

I am 2 years old; I started to go to the pool when I was only 3 months old. In my free time I sing and dance. I love oranges and mandarins.

Kornel

I have been going to the swimming pool since I was 3 months old. I always enjoy it and it is great fun. When I was almost 5 months old, I had a fantastic time on the beach at Krynica Morska.

Leon

I am 4 months old and this is my first time swimming. I really enjoy long baths, rides in my buggy and naps. I am very chatty.

Mateusz

I am 4 years old. I have been swimming since I was 6 months old and on my own since I was 3 years old. I am a happy kindergarten child, I like playing in the fresh air and skiing.

Dolly

When our little heroes were sick or tired, I helped in presenting particular exercises and games.

11

Persons Involved In The Creation Of The Book

Magdalena Dabrowska – co-author

Rehabilitation and swimming are my principal interests. At work I really enjoy the contact with children, which brings great satisfaction. During my free time I relax by skiing or delight in the sounds of the sea. I am a happy mother of 4-year-old Mateusz.

More about my work on www.akademiaruchu.eu

Agnieszka Peszek – editor and co-author

I learnt to swim when I was 5 years old – since then swimming has been my "summer" passion (in the winter it is snowboard and skiing) and I mainly swim front crawl. According to the trainers and instructors who I have met I have an excellent technique.

Ewa Zielinski – author of the chapter on safety

I am a swimming teacher and a lecturer for the Polish Volunteer Water Rescue Service. I love skiing in my free time.

More about the Polish Volunteer Water Rescue Service on **www.wopr.pl**

Andrzej Peszek – photos

Sport and photography are what excite me. Obviously, the connection is sports photography. In winter I go skiing, in summer I spend my time swimming and diving and I take my camera bag everywhere – it weighs a bit but it is worth having at hand.

See more on **www.andrzejpeszek.pl**

Łukasz Drzewinski – consulting on methodology of teaching of swimming

At some stage of my life, I was more swimming than walking. I am a former race swimmer, participant at Olympic Games and multiple winner at the national championships. I have engaged in children's swimming with the birth of my daughter. Playing with her in the water gives me more pleasure than winning gold medals. Besides coaching swimming, I work as a sport manager at Carolina Medical Center.

More on **www.carolina.pl**

Iwona Turant – President of PSPN (the Polish Baby Swimming Association)

Co-author of The Little Swimmers Guidebook, parts of which were used in this book.

Introduction

The birth of a child is a wonderful experience for both mother and father. As parents we try to ensure that our child grows up in the best conditions possible. We take care so that our child will be healthy and happy. Many parents often forget, or simply do not know, that even as a baby and a young child, the appropriate stimulation should be provided for better physical development.

One of the easiest and safest ways to help the child's physical development is to exercise in water and, later on, swimming. On the condition, of course, that those parents know how to do it themselves.

It should be remembered that in the case of small children up to 4 years old, swimming is out of the question and only exercises familiarizing the child with the aquatic environment are ok. Due to these exercises, the child will develop good habits and behavior in water.

Our book is an excellent source of useful information for the parents of children that are younger than 4 years old, for the parents of a child about to start going to the swimming pool, or of a child that already goes to the swimming pool.

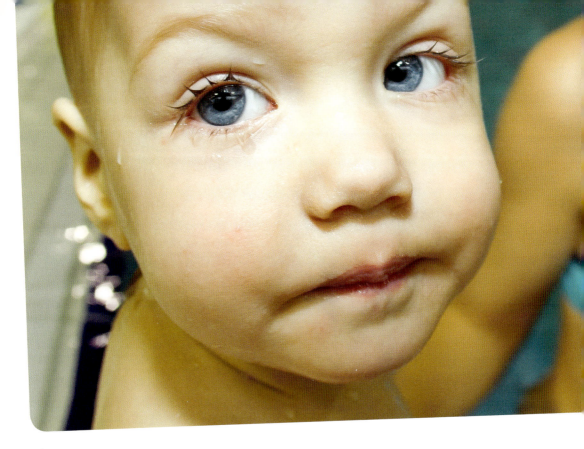

It is also for parents who go to organized classes and also for those who, for various reasons, are unable to participate.

This book would never have been completed without those with whom I had the pleasure of working during its creation. I would like to thank Magda Dabrowska from the Academy of Movement, who shared with me her great knowledge on the subject of exercises in water. I would also like to thank our little heroes and their parents. Thanks to them, particular exercises were performed with children and not with dolls, which undoubtedly provides better illustrations of the exercises.

Wishing you pleasant classes

Agnieszka Peszek

Mother of Julia, who began her adventure with swimming at 3 months old.

The Child In The Water

The Child Swims
– Why Is It The Natural Sequence Of Events?

Swimming is an odd physical activity for a person. It is something for which we are completely unprepared but which we enjoy very much. First, our body is adapted to the vertical position, overcoming the force of gravity and with unrestricted access to air. Secondly, swimming is in the lying position, fully supporting the weight of our body and hindering breathing. How to reconcile this obvious contradiction with the phenomenon of people swimming in

vast numbers? One explanation may be human "defiance" and inclination to accept challenges. The second, perhaps better explanation, is that the "swimming instinct" lies deep in our subconscious mind. If one remembers the time of pregnancy, it may be seen that the previously mentioned contradiction between swimming and our anatomy and physiology does not occur there. The child in the womb is in an aqueous environment unconcerned with gravity or breathing. Unfortunately, we quickly lose this natural "swimming ability" after birth. The quick return of the child to water that we encourage in our book is, as it were, a return to our sleeping natural abilities, all the easier for being the sooner begun.

Why Is It Worth Swimming?

As described above, games in water and learning to swim are in a sense a natural continuation of the development of the child during pregnancy. The aqueous environment, in which the baby is present in the mother's womb, is its first natural environment and, because of its unique characteristics, it perfectly stimulates the development of the child in pregnancy. It is interesting that certain physiological patterns which the child acquires in the mother's womb, such as the ability to open its hands, the child loses after birth in order to regain them after a few months. Movement of children is genetically programmed and, along with the development of the child, to some extent the genetic programming process is liberated. The result is that each of us develops the same regarding the acquisition of the ability to perform particular movements while the experience of being in water has a very positive influence on improving the quality of movement.

Benefits achieved through exercises with children at the pool even from the baby stage are as follows:

- Activities for babies and young children organized in water develop personality and social competence of children through being in a peer group.
- Water enables movement in three planes before the child is capable of moving independently on land. Due to this, movement skill is developed and coordination improves.

- Muscle tissues lying directly under the skin are intensively stimulated by the touch of the parent and water (water flows around the whole body; the resistance of water is felt). It causes the effect of relaxation and regulates muscular tension.
- In water less static muscular work is required (e.g. for overcoming gravity) so it increases the possibilities for dynamic work. The bone is unburdened and the muscles are strengthened.
- Water reacts and corresponds to the movement of the child, but also moves and affects the body of the child itself. The child must counteract changes in position and thus improve its sense of balance.
- Warm water (31-33°C) causes deeper breaths and stimulates the circulation system.
- At the moment of contact with water and because of immersion of the rib cage upwards and downwards, initially breathing is accelerated, after a while it becomes longer and deeper progressively. Inhalation is improved and the muscles involved in breathing are strengthened, which leads to development of the rib cage.
- Comparing a group of children that swim in relation to non-swimmers, the observations confirmed that the "swimmers" adapt better to new situations, have a higher level of self-assurance and independence, have a greater range of

movements and more positive emotional behavior (more frequent smiling, less tears) and also are typified by their greater emotional stability, achieving communication with peer group and more involvement in games.

- Activities in water assist the rehabilitation of children with movement disabilities; integrate physically and also mentally handicapped children with non-handicapped children.

- Swimming strengthens the bonds between children and parents.
- Regularly going to the swimming pool accustoms the child to physical activity.
- Regularly going to the swimming pool increases a child's resistance to infection.
- It is an excellent means of relaxation, physically as well as mentally.
- Children become more self-assured and confident through swimming.

From a medical point of view swimming has a beneficial effect on many of the systems of our body:

The bone-muscular-joint system – the aqueous environment relieves the body (reduces the influence of gravity) and at the same time forms a greater resistance than on land, an even resistance to our movements. This enables the performance of movements in a wide range and with light, even loading.

This assists the muscular development of children, widening the range of movement in the joints and later maintains the bone-joint and muscular system in a good physical condition. Swimming and exercising in water have an excellent effect on the development and maintenance of muscular symmetry and spinal symmetry.

The respiratory system – especially the manner of breathing in water: evenness, depth, and

overcoming the additional resistance associated with the pressure of water on the rib cage are excellent exercise for the respiratory muscles.

The circulation system – swimming is an aerobic, yet enjoyable activity, so it is an excellent exercise for the heart and the circulation system. In addition, the stimulation associated with water pressure and its temperature has a positive effect on circulation in the skin and veins.

The nervous system – swimming provides intensive stimulation equally for surface feeling (contact of skin with water) and also for deeper so-called proprioceptive sensitivity, having an effect on our working joints and muscles; it is an excellent exercise for the sense of equilibrium and finally wonderful relaxation.

Let's Go To The Pool – What Should One Do/Know Before The First Visit?

The child should have positive, well-planned first experience with swimming. Before going to the swimming pool, we should do several things, not necessarily in the order below (more will be said about particular aspects further on in the book):

a. visit the doctor so that the child may be examined to see if there are any reasons for not swimming,

b. consider whether the child is ready to go to the pool,

c. choose appropriate pool and/or swimming school,

d. prepare the child at home for the visit to the pool,

e. acquaint ourselves with the principles of participation in classes at the pool and also find out what we should take with us to the pool.

A Visit To The Doctor

Before we go with the child to the pool, it is necessary to visit the doctor. The majority of swimming schools require a doctor's certificate confirming a lack of contra-indications to participation in classes. If you are not going to go to an organized class, but alone, or the school does not require such a certificate, you should still visit the doctor. The doctor should inform you if your child has reached a suitable stage of development for going to swimming classes.

Generally, contra-indications to swimming are connected with the following ailments:

- Inflammation of the ears, eyes or nose,
- severe infection of the respiratory tract,
- severe infection of the digestive system,
- certain skin diseases,
- sensitivity to ozone or chlorine,
- recurrent and chronic urethral ailment,
- intensified stomach-esophagus reflex,
- some chronic lung ailments,
- recurrent middle ear infection,
- congenital heart, lungs, and urethral defects.

Contra-indications to going to the pool arise if, with regard to the condition of the child, no additional stress should be applied to the child through intensified physical effort or if it is vitally important to limit the risk of infection, because it might cause significant deterioration of the health of the child.

In the case of some vaccinations, one should not take the child to the pool on the day of injection. It is recommended to consult a doctor in these circumstances.

For sanitary reasons, the water in swimming pools is chlorinated or treated with ozone, which may cause short-term reddening of the child's eyes after swimming. Normally, this is not a symptom of any allergy but initial reaction of the mucous membrane of the child to chemical irritation. In order to avoid or diminish this effect one may try applying swimming glasses to a child of 2 years and older and/or apply physiological salt eye drops to the child's eyes.

REMEMBER – Do not take the child to the swimming pool directly after an illness. After some illnesses e.g. following a bladder infection, a longer interval is required before swimming, therefore after a sickness it is always worth consulting a doctor.

IMPORTANT – Dysfunction of motor organs is not a contra-indication to participation in classes.

When To Go To The Pool?

The best age to go to the pool for the first time is at 3 months old. This is because of the development of the child. A correctly developing child already supports its own head. Furthermore, in the third month of life the baby's spine straightens, which means that the child is not so hunched over as in the earlier months. The change occurring at this time in the joints of the child is also important; the joints become rounded, which enables the safe performance of exercises, in the full range of movement.

It would be best if we began the swimming pool adventure no later than at 8 months old. Up to this time the majority of children are not frightened of strangers, which may help in familiarizing oneself not only with water, but also with other children, their carers and with instructors.

Apart from the physical aspect, which determines the possibility of going to the pool, the child's psychological attitude is also important when visiting the pool. Children who are not used to e.g. having water poured on their head may have a problem with accepting this during classes. Therefore, it is very important that at 4-8 weeks before the first visit to the pool, we begin to prepare our child for the water (more on this subject later in the book).

Remember, it is not only the attitude of our child that is significant. We also must be certain that we wish to go to the pool. If going to the pool is stressful for us, our child will sense it. In that case we should think if somebody else should go with the child to the pool, or wait until going to the pool will not worry us.

How To Choose The School And The Swimming Pool?

The increase in the number of companies teaching swimming to babies and children up to 4 years old has made the choice of the appropriate school more complicated.

Going to classes, we must analyze two aspects: the choice of a school and also the choice of a swimming pool. In small towns there may be no choice. In large towns the choice is greater; therefore it is worth choosing the best solution.

Here are several simple indicators for choosing the appropriate school. Find out:

- Do the instructors giving the classes have special training for conducting classes with babies/small children?

- How long do the classes last? It is recommended that classes do not last longer than 30 minutes. Also it is important to know how much time we have before and afterwards for changing.

- At what times are the classes held? Adjust the time of going to the pool to the daily rhythm of the child.

- What children will be going to the classes? It is important that they would be of a similar age. That situation is ideal because the exercises carried out during the class will be best adapted to the movement potential of your child.

- How many participants are there in a group? Apart from the choice of a school, the choice of the appropriate swimming pool is important as well.

In choosing the pool the following factors should be considered:

- Water temperature: Water in the pool should be at 32-33°C for children up to 6 months old and 31-32°C for children from 7-12 months. If the water temperature in the pool is lower, then children of 7-8 months may go to a pool with a water temperature of 29-30°C, on the condition that we cover the child in protective foam. Water temperature can have a significant effect on your child. Too high a temperature may cause overloading of the circulation and respiratory system. Too low a temperature may cause chilling.

- Water quality: Water in the pool should be properly treated.

- Changing room equipment: Being at the pool with a baby, it is important that the changing room should have a baby changing table and a chair or playpen where we can place the child while changing. Alternatively, we must take our own baby carrier to the pool.

- Pool depth: Classes with children are held in shallow pools. The best depth is 1-1.1 m. If we cannot find a pool with exactly those depth measurements, then we may extend the range to 0.7-1.4 m.
- Family changing room: A visit with a small child to the swimming pool is not simple; to make it easier we could go with a family member or friend. In a situation where the companion is of the opposite sex, it is important that we can be in the changing room together.
- Air temperature at the pool (ideally, it should be 2°C higher than the water temperature).
- Check if there is a place where it is possible to sit down with the child, where it is possible to eat, have something to drink, or simply have a rest after the lesson.

How To Prepare At Home For A Visit To The Pool?

A baby may begin preparation for going to the swimming pool when it is 4-8 weeks old. Such preparation should be in an environment familiar to the child, which is at home. "Swimming" at home is intended to familiarize the child with water, to accustom it to the sound of water and the general noise, as well as to changed conditions of the surroundings. Familiarizing the child with splashing, water pouring over the face and also submersion or diving will ensure that the baby does not have problems playing in the water at the pool. The list of example games in the bath is in the section "Exercises in the bath."

IMPORTANT! If it is compulsory to wear a swimming cap at the pool, accustom the child to wearing a cap and also to the sight of you in a cap.

You can actually prepare your child from birth, because it is then that you start to bathe the child. In the beginning bathe the child in a small baby bath, from 4-8 weeks change it for a large bath, if you have one. To better prepare the child to go to the pool, reduce the water temperature in the bath to 34-35°C.

What Should We Know Going To The Pool?

What should we know before we go to the pool?

a. Familiarize yourself with rules in force at the pool which you have chosen.

Particularly important information for you is:

- Is it compulsory to wear swimming caps?
- May an accompanying person come into the changing room or enter the pool with us? If so, then on what basis and how should they be dressed? What are the charges?
- What clothing must be worn while swimming? This particularly applies to men. At the majority of pools one may not go in wearing shorts.

b. Acquaint yourself with the layout of rooms at the pool so that you do not make a mistake on your first visit. Problems with finding changing rooms, showers, and the entrance to the pool may be stressful for you and also for the child.

c. Do not apply cream or oil to the child before going to the swimming pool to avoid the risk of the child slipping in your hands. It also contaminates the water in the pool.

d. Feeding before entering the pool should be at least 30 minutes before the class. Children who are breastfed are an exception.

e. Choose a suitable time for participating in classes − arrange the visit to the pool according to your child's rhythm. If your child sleeps at different times, on the day of the visit to the pool put it to bed earlier, so that it will not be sleepy during the class.

f. Bathe yourself and the child before and after the class in the shower!

Additional useful information:

a. Going to the pool with a child does not require you to know how to swim. The class takes place in shallow water. Remember though, if a visit to the pool is very stressful for you, it might be worth considering that the child goes to the pool with somebody else because your stress will be passed on to the child.

b. Sometimes a child has a bad day, is teething, or is simply feeling grumpy. Consider then whether it is worth taking the child to a class. A visit to the pool should be enjoyable.

c. During classes the parent/carer performs the exercises with the child – **NOT THE IN-STRUCTOR**.

d. One does not eat in the changing rooms.

e. Put on the bathing costume and diapers at the pool – **NOT AT HOME**.

List Of Things For The Pool

The list of things necessary to take to the pool is long; therefore, when going to the pool for the first time it is worth writing down everything. Before we go, we should check that we have everything:

- a swimming costume for you,
- diapers for the child for swimming or a swimming costume if it no longer uses diapers,
- normal diapers if the child uses them,
- goggles for an older child,
- slippers for the parent,

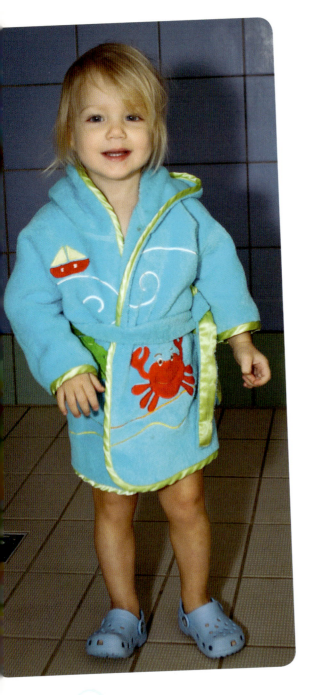

- slippers for a walking child (if it is winter, and the child has tights, it is worth having two pairs of slippers),
- a towel for the parent,
- a towel for the child – better two, or a towel and dressing gown,
- baby carrier – for as much as one may take to the pool,
- cosmetics – soap, shampoo for the parent, soap, baby oil, cream for the child,
- a dryer – if there are no dryers at the pool,
- swimming caps – if they are required,
- bags for wet clothes – for convenience,
- second set of clothes for the child – just in case,
- food, drink – for afterwards,
- a toy, a small book so that the child has something to occupy them with when you are changing,
- a swimming pool pass.

The First Visit To The Pool

The first visit to the pool is often stressful; Normally more so for the parent than the child. To make things easier, here is an example of a visit to the pool:

1. Leave your street clothing in a changing room.
2. Change yourself and the child into swimming costumes. While changing, it is convenient to strap the child into the baby carrier or, if it sits, put it into a baby chair (if available in the changing room)

3. **REMEMBER** – never leave the child on a changing mat without an adult by its side. Children who still have not moved may do so for the first time just when you are not beside them.

4. Take off jewelry and watches. Do not place the locker key on your wrist.

5. Slippers are worn in the swimming pool complex. If the child already walks, buy it a pair of slippers for the pool.

6. If required, put a cap on and put one on the child.

7. Before going to the pool, wash yourself and the child. Going into the pool without first washing may cause the transfer to the water of microorganisms, which may be harmful to your health and the health of other pool users.

8. Do NOT enter the pool with the child using the ladder. Normally classes with children are organized in the shallow end where entry is easy. If there is no shallow end, ask somebody to help you – first enter the pool yourself and ask your helper to pass the child to you. The method of leaving the pool is presented later in the book.

9. During the class the child may not have anything in its mouth.

10. After leaving the pool, do not remove the diapers from the child anywhere in the vicinity of the pool. In the event that the child has soiled diapers, everything would flow into the water.

11. **REMEMBER** – after leaving the water, carefully wash yourself and the child. Then rub the appropriate cream onto the child – the swimming pool may dry out the skin.

12. Dry your head and the child's head with a towel. Wipe the child's ears with the towel.

13. In the changing room, or after leaving the changing room, dry the child and yourself thoroughly with a blow dryer. It is best to wait 20-30 minutes before leaving the swimming pool complex – especially in winter.

Exercises In The Bath

Preparing the child for classes in the water may begin from the first bath.

Proper preparation should take place 4-8 weeks before the first classes.

Preparing the child for classes, parents may perform exercises in various configurations:

- in a small bath independently,
- in a small bath with help of a third person,
- in a large bath together with the child,
- in a large bath together with the child with help of a third person,
- independent exercises of the child in a large bath.

Various toys may be used for playing in the bath – typical toys for the bath are: balls, watering can, foam puzzle or special bath markers for use after the bath.

Familiarizing The Child With Water

Familiarizing the child with water should begin slowly with wetting the legs then the stomach and the back. If the child is independent i.e. sits and, better still, stands, we may let it define the rate of wetting. The child will sit in the water itself when it is ready.

Hold the child securely.

Slowly wet the child, giving it time to relax. Begin immersion with the legs and next wet its back.

REMEMBER – Placing the child in water, we must support it firmly and securely. If we are afraid that the child is a bit too slippery in the bath, we should buy a special mat for the bottom of the bath.

A child becomes tense during stressful moments. Allow the child to become accustomed to the new situation, to relax before we begin, to really acquaint the child with water.

Getting into the water with the child, if possible ask a partner to pass the child to you when you are already sitting steadily in the bath. If this is not possible, carefully get into the bath with the child, taking care not to wet it.

...and then slowly wet a larger part of the child's legs.

An older child that is at least sitting can be seated on the edge of the bath so that it may freely kick the water. Obviously, we hold the child securely the whole time.

When sitting, hold the child in such a manner that only its toes touch the water...

Pouring Water Over The Child

To wet the child, do not completely immerse it at once. Begin by slowly pouring water over the child. A baby is not accustomed to intensive contact with water, at the beginning of the bath we may pour water from the palm of the hand and if the child is afraid, sprinkle it with drops of water. The intensity of pouring water over the child should depend upon the muscular tension of the child among other things. We pour water over the child in such a way that it sees the source of water and is able to stretch out its hands. If a child is older we may use a watering can, a mug or other container.

Pouring water over the child, we begin from the feet and finish at its head.

We may "sprinkle" the child...

or a watering can.

pour water with an open palm...

We begin pouring with the legs, then we pour water on the stomach...

and then on the head.

positions, equally when it lies on its sto-mach. We may pour water on its back using the "goblet" grip, which is moving the palms of our hands under the head of the child; for stability the thumbs must be directed up-wards and wrists must be together. In this position we need the help of a partner to pour water on the child.

When we pour water on the head, the child reacts by closing its eyes.

Also bathing with the child, we may pour water over it. We can do this, holding the child with its back to us...

We may pour water on the child in various

or facing us – then we see the face of the child and its reaction, which is safer, particularly at the beginning.

If we wish to vary the child's exercises, we may place the child on our forearm and with our palm grasp a further arm of the child ("carousel grip"). We give delicate back support, because at this age a baby is still not completely developed.

We also pour water on older children; we may encourage them to pour water over themselves with a watering can or even with a shower.

Lying On The Back In Water

Lying on their back in water is a big problem for many children. Therefore, it is worth acquainting the child with this position in the familiar home environment.

From the moment it begins to turn itself on its stomach, the child is unwilling to lie on its back. This is because it has acquired new motor abilities and wishes to make use of them all the time — as a child that sits is unwilling to lie down. When it stands, it will no longer wish to sit. Older children who already sit also have a problem with lying on their backs. For them, too, lying is not attractive.

An additional problem for some children may be having water in their ears. Remember: if water gets into a child's ears, it is sufficient after bathing to carefully dry the ears with a towel, or to turn the child on one side and then the other, so that the water may trickle out.

There are several grips or holds, which one may use in the bath, to securely hold the child in a position on its back.

We lay the child on its back, with one hand we support its head (back of the head), using the other hand to stabilize its chin.

47

We may do the same exercise with older children.

Instead of by the chin we may prop the child at the height of the sacral bone. We support the child alternating one hand with the other – this teaches the child balance and lying on the water.

We may also support the child with one hand. For stabilization the child may support itself on the bottom of the bath.

Alternatively, we can support the child under the back of the head.

We may perform the same exercise, if we are in the bath together with the child. The child lies on the palm of the hand, which is under the head of the baby. If the child is anxious, we may rest the other hand on the rib cage from above (this hold is called "waterbed").

If we are able to support the child securely with one hand, we may take a toy with the other hand so that the child may follow it by sight or, if older, stretch out to reach it.

The next hold is "towing": we lay the child on its back on the palms of the hands, with thumbs upwards. The head of the child is supported on our wrists. In addition, we may gently move the child to the side. Obviously, we make this movement very slowly. Movement of the child causes alternating relaxa- tion and tightening of the muscles on both sides of the chest. The child learns to keep its balance and also becomes accustomed to the splashing of water.

Older children may lie in water alone, exer- cising additionally e.g. submerging their head.

Leg Stimulation On The Back

Leg exercises may be performed in various positions.

If help is available, we may place the child on our palms, thumbs upwards, the second person helps the child move its legs.

We may change the hold to "cradle" and place the child on the forearm, supporting the child with the extended arm and with the free hand stimulate the work of hands; or, for example, show the child a toy, which will attract its attention so that it will reach out for it.

With older children that already sit stably, kicking may be practiced sitting in the bath.

The work of the legs may also be stimulated being in the bath together with the child.

For variety we may throw a toy into the bath for the child to kick. Use of toys causes the child to concentrate upon them, which is excellent concentration training for the baby.

Lying On The Stomach

One of the basic holds that enable stable lying on the stomach is the so called "goblet". We lay the child on the palms of our hands, with the thumbs upwards, wrists together – which prevents the child from submerging its head unless allowed to do so.

Important! Do not pull the child out of the water in this position.

This hold may also be used when we are in the bath with the child. We may move the child towards us or away from us; we may also make gentle sideways movements. This variety influences relaxation of the child and activates leg work.

When we draw the child towards us, we may try to make eye contact to exercise the child's concentration.

Leg Stimulation Lying On The Stomach

It is best to work on leg exercises when we have a second person to help who can work alternatively on both of the baby's legs. In this situation, we use the "goblet" hold, and the second person moves the child's legs. While performing this exercise, it should be remembered that the movement should begin in the hips and not to bend the child's knees too much. Try to help the child move both legs fully.

Also remember that exercises are performed delicately and slowly within the range of joint movement possible for the child. Allow the child to make spontaneous independent movements. During this we say, for example, 'hop, hop' so that the child would associate movement with a given trigger word.

Lying On The Stomach On A Floating Board

Lying on the stomach on a board is an excellent exercise supporting stable lying on the stomach and proper support for the hands.

If we have a swimming board at home, we may place the child on it and, for example, gently rock it sideways.

Older children may practice making bubbles.

If we have help, we may also exercise leg movement.

Lying On The Back On A Board

On the board one can also exercise lying on the back, including rocking sideways. During the exercises, the baby loosens the pelvis and also activates the stomach muscles due to raising the legs and their alternate work.

Lying with legs swinging.

Active Breathing Out And Diving

Holding our breath at the moment of submerging the face and actively breathing out into the water are two abilities that are essential for learning to swim later, which we may begin to exercise at the stage of baby games in the bath.

Sometimes children do not close their mouths when they put their heads under water. Do not worry as the young child (up to about 6 months) automatically closes its respiratory tract to exclude water.

Diving submersion in the bath: we try to feel the breathing rhythm of the child's rib cage – when the child breathes in – and when the child breathes out.

1.　　　　　2.　　　　　3.　　　　　4.

1. At the moment of beginning breathing out, we submerge the child, pulling it towards us and downwards.
2. During submersion, the child first moves vertically, later horizontally.
3. During submersion, the child has closed eyes and mouth.
4. A happy child after the first dive in its life.

57

Actively breathing out in the water.

ATTENTION!

1. We talk to the child. We think of a key word that will precede diving so that the child may prepare itself and not be surprised, i.e. '1, 2, 3, dive'.
2. Practice diving so that the child has a wet head and face to be better prepared for submersion.

Making bubbles – we can practice different variations with the child:

- gentle blowing: making foam bubbles,
- blowing out air at different depths,
- blowing out different amounts of air,
- speaking and singing while breathing out.

Additional Games And Exercises

Becoming Acquainted With One's Own Body

For children it is important to quickly learn how their body is arranged. One of the elements of this process is crossing the central line of the body – practice this by encouraging children younger than 4.5 months to cross the central bodyline reaching for a toy (it also applies to older children if they do not do this).

Joining Hands

We guide movement carefully through the range of joint movements that the child possesses at the given stage of development. Exercise stimulates synchronization of the brain hemispheres and also teaches symmetrical lying on the back. This exercise is particularly important for children of less than 3 months old or for those children that do not join hands by themselves.

Attempt To Attract The Child's Attention

Here we exercise concentrating the attention of the child on an object. For the youngest children we use black and white toys.

Exercising with a ball: For variety we may use toys with different textures, e.g. balls with studded surfaces to massage the child during the playtime in the bath.

Play In The Bath

Time spent in the bath should be divided between time for exercises and playtime. In order to give variety to the time spent with the child in the bath, we may use many interesting "natural" and bought toys. In the bath the child may, for example...

... play with washable felt tip crayons.

... play with puzzles that stick to tiles.

... play with foam.

... play with toys, little water containers, etc. A lot of blowing, e.g. through a straw, to encourage the child to wet the mouth and the head.

Safety

Principles Of Safe Bathing – Volunteer Water Rescue Service Advice

Principles of safe bathing include behavior before entering the water, during bathing, and after leaving the water. For bathing to be safe, parents with the child at the swimming pool should observe the following 10 guidelines:

1. Ask the doctor whether the child may participate in swimming at the pool.
2. Do not feed the child directly before or after bathing.
3. Ensure the psychological and physical comfort of the child while playing in the water.
4. Directly before bathing, cool the child's body with water.
5. Check whether the child has any object in its mouth that might cause choking.
6. Acquaint yourself with and observe the rules of the swimming pool.
7. Comply with the instructions by the instructor running the class and the lifeguard.
8. Do not leave the child without the care of an adult.
9. Enter and leave the water safely.
10. In the event of an accident, immediately inform the instructor running the class and the Volunteer Water lifeguard.

First Aid For The Baby Not Breathing, Choking, Or Choking On An Object

During the class in the water, the baby may stop breathing or choke. It is connected with insufficient development of the respiratory tract and anatomical differences. The question arises: "Why are adults afraid to rescue a baby?" The answer seems to be obvious. Differences in physique and typical ailments of children cause adults to worry about giving incorrect first aid and perhaps doing harm. They do not undertake lifesaving activities and transfer this obligation to the medical service. It should be clearly emphasized that it is most important for the health and life of the victim that lifesaving activity is begun within the first four minutes after an incident has occurred. The earlier the life-saving procedures start, the greater is the chance that the victim will survive and fully recover.

The resuscitation procedures for babies are presented below.

By **resuscitation** we mean the restoration of the respiratory and/or circulation system.

Outline of basic resuscitation procedures for children:

CHECK SAFETY

If the child does not react, **SHOUT FOR HELP LOUDLY**

CLEAR THE RESPIRATORY TRACT AND CHECK BREATH

If the child does not breathe properly, **PERFORM 5 RESCUE BREATHS**

If there is no sign of life: **30 PRESSES ON THE RIB CAGE**

2 INHALATIONS

After 1 minute and unsuccessful Circulation-Breathing Resuscitation, call emergency responders.

Precise description of particular actions

Safety Evaluation

A parent giving aid (rescuer), prior to beginning resuscitation must ensure their own safety and the safety of the injured baby.

Assess accident location and eliminate all dangers in relation to the rescuer and the victim.

For one's own safety and that of the victim, the rescuer should use protective gloves.

Assess Consciousness

In order to assess consciousness for a baby, it is necessary to observe reactions to stimulus.

To do this, touch the feet or the inside of the palm of the hand. Never hit a baby.

Ensure That You Have Someone To Help. Shout For Help Loudly.

If there is no reaction to stimulus, ensure that you have someone to help that is designated a person who will remain with the rescuer and, if necessary, summon help.

If there is nobody nearby, the rescuer should shout loudly for help.

Clear The Respiratory Tract And Check Breathing.

In order to assess breathing, a person giving aid should clear the respiratory tract of the baby; lay the baby on a hard surface in a "sniffing" position. To do this, place your hand or, for example, diapers under the baby's back. This automatically causes bending back of the head and pointing the nose upwards. Check if there is anything in the mouth cavity. If there is a visible foreign body or stomach content, it is necessary to clean the mouth cavity. One may do this by insertion of two fingers wrap-

ped in gauze into the mouth of the baby. Never ever explore the mouth cavity with the fingers, if nothing is visible.

If the mouth cavity is clear, lean over the baby and check whether it is breathing properly. Place your ear against the mouth and nose of the victim.

From the corner of the eye we observe the movements of the rib cage and on our cheek we try to detect the movement of air. If the baby is not breathing properly, it is necessary to ventilate the lungs.

5 Rescue Breaths

To perform 5 rescue inhalations, it is necessary to bend over the baby, and with one's mouth closely cover the child's mouth and nose, then blow air in such a way that only the rib cage rises. Next, the rescuer should remove their mouth from the mouth and nose of the child and observe whether the rib cage falls. If so, it means that we have performed a proper inhalation and the action should be repeated 5 times. If as a result of this action proper breathing is restored, we apply the safety position.

If we observe no sign of life, it is necessary to begin circulation-respiration resuscitation.

Cardiopulmonary Resuscitation (CPR) 30 to 2

To begin CPR, the rescuer should place two fingers (fore and middle fingers) on the rib cage of the baby. Press the rib cage 30 times then perform 2 artificial inhalations. It is necessary to give attention to the quality of the pressure applied. Compression of the rib cage amounts to at least 1/3 of its front-back dimensions in all children, i.e. about 4 cm in the case of babies. Frequency of compressions on the ribcage should amount to 100-120 times a minute.

Calling Help

After a minute of unsuccessful resuscitation, it is necessary to call an ambulance, telephoning the emergency numbers. In most countries: 112 or 911.

If it is not possible to effectively summon help, it is recommended to "run for help with the child."

IMPORTANT:

The rescuer continues resuscitation to the moment of:

- return of vital functions to the baby,
- arrival of an ambulance,
- or exhaustion of the rescuer.

Placing The Baby In A Safe Position

Hold the baby on the hands with the head turned away and directed downwards. That position prevents the respiratory tract from being obstructed and protects against choking. Monitor vital signs and in the event of their disappearance, undertake CPR.

Choking And Inhalation Of Liquid Or Solid Matter Into Airways.

Treatment of choking in babies needs assessment of consciousness and effectiveness of cough.

While playing in the water, choking, inhalation of fluid, or choking on some object often occurs. Also objects taken into the mouth of the baby may constitute the cause of obstruction of the respiratory tract.

If the baby coughs and the cough is effective – then urge the baby to cough, continuously monitoring life signs. It is a great mistake to restrain effective coughing by slapping the coughing person on the back.

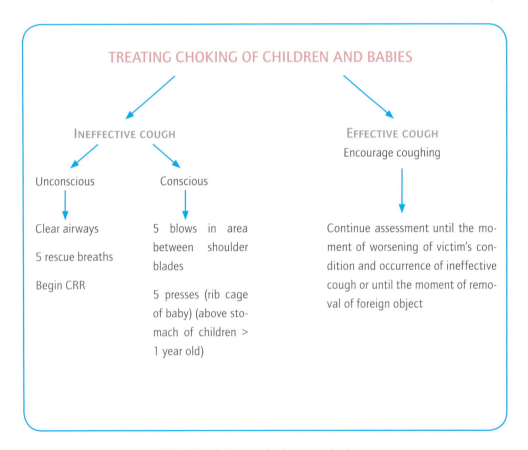

TREATING CHOKING OF CHILDREN AND BABIES

INEFFECTIVE COUGH

Unconscious

Clear airways

5 rescue breaths

Begin CRR

Conscious

5 blows in area between shoulder blades

5 presses (rib cage of baby) (above stomach of children > 1 year old)

EFFECTIVE COUGH
Encourage coughing

Continue assessment until the moment of worsening of victim's condition and occurrence of ineffective cough or until the moment of removal of foreign object

CRR = Circulation-respiration resuscitation

Situation I – Cough Ineffective, Baby conscious

If the cough becomes ineffective but the baby is conscious – then sit down with the baby and lay it on your forearm, along the body central line. The face of the victim should be turned towards the floor; in addition, we hold the lower limbs of the baby with our arm. Slap up to 5 times in the area between the shoulder blades. After each blow, observe whether the foreign body has been expelled from the respiratory tract. If not, then in the same sitting position turn the baby onto its back so that its face is directed upwards, but the head is placed definitely below the level of the heart. Place two fingers: the forefinger and the middle finger on the rib cage and press five times. After each application of pressure, check the content of the mouth cavity. Such double sequences, that is, up to 5 slaps in the area between the shoulder blades and up to 5 applications of pressure above the stomach, may be applied up to 5 times. If the treatment procedures are ineffective, that is, we do not clear the respiratory tract, proceed to CPR.

Situation II – Cough Ineffective, Baby Unconscious

If the cough is ineffective and the baby is unconscious, apply resuscitation procedure schedule.

Finally At The Pool

Entering The Pool

There are several ways for the child to enter the pool.

a. Go down the steps, which is the easiest and the safest way.

For children that are frightened of the surroundings.

For braver children.

b. Without the steps, with the aid of a second person.

The person standing on the edge holds the child by the rib cage from behind and passes the child to the person standing in the water. The person standing in the water grasps the rib cage of the child from the front. Not by the shoulders which may slip away.

This is the way we pass the child to the person standing on the edge.

c. Without steps, independently (for children that already sit by themselves);

We seat the child beside us on the edge.

Enter the water slowly, securing the child with one's arms against falling into the water and against leaning and falling backwards.

Place the hands in such a way to grip the child from the side by the rib cage with one and then with the other hand.

When already standing steadily facing the child, we may gently draw it on to the surface of the water.

77

Depending on the age of the child, we may enter the water having the child in position:

a. "Heart to heart", that is facing us. It is recommended in the case of small children, that is, less than 6 months old, especially at the first visit to the pool.

In the case of older children, the child is supported on the hip of the parent.

b. With the back to the parent, the child is supported under its bottom in half sitting pose.

c. The child enters water on its own, depending on whether it is able to walk.

It is important that while holding the child, one has the ability to support it if it slips.

Before going into the water with the child, we try to prepare it. We may, for example, sit on the edge and slowly begin to wet the child by splashing its legs.

79

Methods Of Holding The Child In The Pool

Moving in the water with the child, we may use the grips recommended for entering the water and also holding the child by the rib cage not from behind but "face to face".

Holding The Child By The Rib Cage Not From Behind But "Face To Face"

Hold the child from the sides, by the rib cage, so that the palms of your hands are on the child's back and the thumbs are to the front of the rib cage. It is important that children hold their heads up firmly.

In this position we may freely lift the child. By holding the child by the rib cage, we avoid the risk of the child's shoulders slipping through our hands.

Similarly, we may hold the child from the rear, which is holding the rib cage with the fingers from the front and with the thumbs behind the back.

We may move around the pool also holding the child on one of our hips.

Preparing The Child For Going Into The Pool

Before immersing the child in the water, prepare it for contact with the water. We may do this in two ways: wet it on the edge or when it is already in the water.

We sit the child in front of us, between our legs. Firstly, we pour water on its legs with our hand, and then we hold its legs and splash them against the water.

Pour water on the child just like during the preparation at home, beginning with the legs and finishing on the head.

This procedure may be performed in the water – we may pour water on the child from a watering can, holding the child using the "carousel hold"

or splash the water on by hand.

Holds And Exercises For The Child On Its Stomach

Exercises on the stomach are generally pleasant for the child. The child sees the world around it and, depending on how it is held, it is able to see the parent. Particular attention should be given to:

Drinking water. Many children drink the water in the pool, which is very easy on the stomach position. Water from the pool in small quantities is not harmful, but you should discourage the child from doing it.

Uncontrolled submersion of the mouth, which may be unpleasant for the child.

"Goblet"

It is a very good hold, particularly for children of less than 6 months old (we may use it on 3-4-months-old children), when our child is still unable to support its head for very long. This hold may also be used with older children, but not too long because it limits the child's free movement. In this hold, as in every other one, if it is physically possible, we try to have our face at the same level as the face of the child so that we may maintain unrestricted eye contact.

if the head of the child falls, if the child is tired, its mouth is still not submerged because it is supported on our wrists.

This hold enables us to alter the distance between the child and us. We may hold the child further from us or nearer to us. We teach the child to blow into the water or to kiss.

For variety, we may also make gentle movements sideways.

Thumb from above, a palm under the rib cage, wrists together.

To ensure the hold is stable and safe for the child, place the palms of the hand widely under the child's rib cage, with thumbs directed upwards, and place the wrists together.

In this position the child feels safe because it sees its parent for the whole time. Furthermore,

Child On The Stomach Laid Over The Shoulder Of An Adult

Lay the child on its stomach, so that the child's rib cage is supported by our shoulder. The child's hands should be forwards. Hold the child by the legs and help it kick up and down.

In this position the child has free hands and can splash the water with them.

The same exercise may be done with older children, then we try not to help with leg kicking.

Older children may be persuaded to submerge the head and practice breathing out underwater.

The child should be slightly leaning towards the water.

We do not see the face of the child therefore we must watch it all the time.

87

Sloping
(angle: 45°)

We hold the child in such a way that the palms of our hands would be on the rib cage from the front and the thumbs would be on the sides. This position enables holding the child to the side of the parent, which enables checking that the child e.g. does not drink the water. This hold is recommended for children over 5 months.

For children who do not yet hold their heads steadily, we recommend directing one's fingers in the direction of the child's lower jaw so that if the child's head falls, it will be supported on our fingers.

Hold Under The Rib Cage (So-called "Carousel")

Place the child on the forearm, and with the hand hold the child behind the forearm. This hold is recommended if the child already has sufficiently developed shoulders which normally occurs at approx. 6 months. The grip must not be too tight so as not to stop the flow of blood in the veins.

Hold the child under the arm with the palm of the hand.

In this hold we may "massage the back" of the child.

This hold enables us to freely and safely move the child over the surface of the water. Additionally, it gives great freedom of movement to the child.

Furthermore, having a free hand we may activate leg exercise.

"Island"

We support the child on our forearm, with the child's arms placed on it. Our hands are straight and joined. Our hands must be sufficiently close to each other so that the child does not slide into the water.

In this hold the child does not lie flat on the water. It may be vertical or at an angle to the surface of the water.

91

This hold may cause some difficulty with an active child.

The parent may have the impression that the child is sliding away.

If we are able to securely hold the child, we may splash the water in front of the child with the hand.

On Bent Elbow

We lay the child on our bent elbow, which lies on the water. If the pool is shallow, we must crouch a bit. The child is supported on the parent's arm, from the other side by the forearm. This hold is specified for children who can hold their heads up with stability.

In this position the child has complete freedom of movement, or it may, for instance, splash with its hands.

Lying On The Palms Of The Parent – "Waiter's Tray"

This hold is used if the weight of the child and the width of the rib cage enable supporting the child on one hand. Lay the child on its stomach, face towards you, on the palm of your hand. Keep the free hand close to the child, in case of need.

For a child of less than 6 months old, apart from the assurance of the second hand, there should be no need of additional "support."

In the case of older, very mobile children, if we are worried that the child might slide away from us or is simply already too heavy for us, then we no longer use this exercise.

"Basket"

This hold is a good exercise for stabilizing the body. The position is similar to that in the "goblet" hold but this hold is somewhat lower. The child is facing the parent. We grip the child either side at the height of the rib cage. The child has complete freedom of movement in the shoulders.

For variation of the exercises we may rock the child sideways and lightly lift it up and down.

Hands Stimulation – "Crawl"

When we are completely confident with the "carousel" position, we may introduce exercises stimulating the work of the hands, the so-called "crawl". Holding the child with the palm of the hand or the forearm and helping it to make movements approximate to the "crawl".

Holding the child by the forearm, we make circular movements.

In the case of older children, we urge the child to do the exercises without help.

Hands Stimulation – Reaching For Toys

We hold the child from behind by the rib cage or by the hips or lay the child on our forearm, so that it may move its hands freely. Throw a floating toy in front of you and then swim towards it so that the child may reach out to it. We may modify the exercise and lift the child so that it can reach downwards for the toy. One may also use a toy that sinks in water so that the child would try to reach it under the water.

Hands may be stimulated alternately: right, left; one may also ask the child to use both hands at the same time or also first right then left or away from the body so that the child would cross the central line of its own body.

Hands Stimulation – Splashing

Splashing is an excellent exercise not only for the work of the hands, but also to familiarize the child with water.

This exercise may be done using various holds. The best hold is "island".

Legs Stimulation

The "carousel" grip enables us to also perform exercises assisting legwork development. The child may kick its legs by itself – we may help the child by moving it over the surface of the water, which with the majority of children causes leg movement. If the child does not kick its legs, we can help it with the free hand.

Leg kicking may also be done with the child placed on our arm.

Wetting One Cheek And Then The Other Cheek

We hold the child by the rib cage, facing towards us and then lean the child first to one side and then the other, so that it wets one cheek and then the other. To begin with, we do this exercise very slowly and we try to wet the cheeks delicately. The more the child is familiar with water, the quicker the movements may be, and then besides the cheek we try also to wet the ear.

The exercise is preparation for diving. We accustom the child to the feeling of water on particular parts of the face. It teaches closing the mouth and actively breathing out into the water.

Facing the parent

With the back to the parent

At the next stage, we place the child on its side submerging successively: an ear, a cheek and next the mouth so that feeling water the child closes its mouth.

While doing the exercises, one may encourage the child to make bubbles.

At the next stage we combine breathing out into the water with submersion of a cheek and the mouth.

When we see that the child controls the breathing out of air, then we may do diving in this position. This may be done when the child is facing us and after that with its back towards us.

Bubbles

Among the games for the swimming pool, that most frequently makes children smile, is making bubbles. Making bubbles is very important because it encourages actively breathing out. Making bubbles is an excellent exercise for children with reduced muscular tension because it teaches controlled closing of the mouth. Bubbles may be made in various positions:

In the "goblet" hold

With the child beside you (45° angle)

Or wetting the cheeks "face to face"

Holds And Exercises On The Back

Holds and exercises performed on the back sometimes cause problems. Firstly, in this position the child normally does not see the parent, which may be stressful for the child. Additionally, many children are not accustomed to water pouring into their ears.

Therefore, if the child reacts by crying to exercises on the back, introduce them gradually, giving the child time to become accustomed.

107

Cheek To Cheek

Place the child on its back, supporting its head on your shoulder. If the pool is not deep enough, it is necessary to bend your knees for the child to lie on the water. One may hold the child by the rib cage from above or by the leg (by a thigh, then a knee or a calf).

Support the child on your shoulder.

You may hold it by the leg...

... or by the rib cage.

During the exercises the child should lie on the water. If the pool is too shallow, we must bend to our knees.

If the child lies steadily, we may take our hand from its rib cage ...

... and stimulate the legs to kicking. The movement of the legs must come from the hips, do not straighten the child's leg at the knee – it must come naturally.

109

On The Back – "Towing" By The Shoulders

Exercises to accustom the child to lying on its back: The child is held by the shoulders in such a manner that the fingers of both hands support the back of the child and the thumbs are directed upwards. This hold enables us to hold the child at a distance or draw it towards us, and if the pool is shallow, to show ourselves to the child.

Fingers under the back, thumbs upwards. The exercise may be done on straight arms...

... or with arms bent.

We may also show ourselves to the child.

This hold also enables us to make sideways movements.

Stimulating The Arms – Stretching Out Arms To Toys

The "cheek to cheek" position is an excellent position for stimulating the hands, particularly for children younger than one year old. With one hand we hold the child, with the other we hold the toy. We try to encourage the child to reach out with its hands.

Stimulating The Legs

The legs may be stimulated in various holds e.g. "towing" or "cheek to cheek". The exercise consists of kicking and has a very good influence on leg development.

The child may kick by itself or with our help. We may also vary the game by throwing a floating toy for the child to kick.

In the position "towing" the child can kick by itself.

In the position "cheek to cheek" the child can kick by itself or with our help.

Kicking the water in the position "cheek to cheek"

To encourage the child to kick we may use a toy.

115

Lying On The Water

Lying on the water is an important preparatory element of learning to swim. In order to teach it, one uses holds applied in the bath.

Lay the child on the water, support the head with one hand and use the other hand to provide support under the chin.

One may lay older children on the palms of hands (thumbs upwards).

Combinations

The holds shown in the previous sections may be made in various combinations.

Transition From The Stomach To The Back And From The Back To The Stomach

Lay the child on the forearm and hold it with one hand. With the other hand lay the child on its back.

Gently lift the child upwards.

Slowly place the child upright in a vertical position.

Slowly lay the child on the hand that was on the back. Hold the child's stomach with the second hand.

118

Finally At The Pool

The child may swim for a while on its back.

Once again place the child in the vertical position.

And then lay the child on the hand, which is on the child's stomach.

This combination may be repeated many times.

Jumping Into The Water And Diving

Jumping into the water and diving is an important element of familiarizing the child with water and learning to swim later. However, here the basic principle of children in the water classes applies: **Do nothing by using force!**

Jump Into The Water From The Sitting Position With Transition In "Goblet" Hold

Seat the child on the pool edge. If the baby is unable to sit independently, do not do this exercise without assisting the baby while sitting. Overburdening the spine should be avoided and therefore the child must be continuously supported. When the child sits on the edge, support it with elbows on the edge. Remember that a child that is unable to sit independently cannot sit upright – but must be slightly hunched forward. When we are ready to make the jump, gently lean the child forwards and then slowly draw the child onto the water surface. Pulling the child onto the water surface, place your hands from the child's sides to the stomach. The fingers are at the height of the rib cage, the thumbs are extended.

When the child is sitting, one supports one's elbows on the edge of the pool.

Slowly lean the child forward.

Place the hands under the stomach of the child, moving to the "goblet" grip and pull the child to the water.

This jump may equally finish with a dive. Remember, if the child is submerged underwater, pull it to you.

Jump Into The Water – Parent's Hand Under The Rib Cage

Stand to the side of the child, support it from the front by the shoulder; with the other hand protect the child's head or back so that the child does not tip backwards. Slowly lean the child forwards so that the child dives stomach first.

ATTENTION! Before making a dive, always check whether anyone is standing behind you so that the child does not swim into anybody.

Jump Into Open Hands

We place our hand on the water or, if the child is afraid or uncertain, we raise our hand to the height of the child's stomach. With the other hand we support the child's shoulder, preventing the child from leaning backwards or falling over. The child should lean forwards itself and fall into our hands lying on the water. As soon as the child falls, we swim away from the edge with the child on one hand and securing it with the other hand placed on its back.

Jump On Open Hands

We stand in front of the child, placing both hands on the water or, if the child is afraid, above the water. We encourage the child to jump into the water.

127

Jump With Protection Of A Second Person

Seat the child on the edge of the pool. The person in the water places their hands on the water. The person securing the child stands behind the child holding it by the shoulders and gently leaning the child forwards, encouraging it to jump into the hands of the person in the water while making sure that the child does not tip over backwards and strike its head.

Standing Jump

A standing child may jump into the water in the standing position.

Young children should do this with the support of the parent.

Older children may jump independently.

Diver

An important part of playing at the swimming pool is diving. Many parents wait uneasily for the moment when the child submerges itself completely in the water. If this makes you very nervous, give the child to the instructor. If you are at the pool without an instructor and you are very nervous, do not do anything by compulsion. Remember that the child senses our stress and may associate a visit to the pool with something stressful. Before diving, it is necessary to give the child a signal that it is about to dive, e.g. '1, 2, 3 dive' and wet the child's head and face.

Diver in "carousel" hold with water poured on the head.

To prepare the child, pour water from a watering can.

131

Exercises By The Edge

Spring

For children the game of pushing off the sides of the pool is very important. This exercise teaches work of the legs – that is automatically bending and straightening the legs. After pushing off, one may change to lying on the back.

Swimming to the side

Pushing off

Swimming away from the side

Towing

Swimming To The Edge

It is the important element of **SAVING ONESELF** for the child.

Placing the child on its stomach, supporting it from behind by the side, swim to the edge. Encourage the child to reach out and grasp the edge.

Older children may dive while swimming to the edge, and, if they already can, swim to the edge by themselves.

Getting Out Of The Water

A very important ability which the child should master is independently getting out of the pool. It is the next important element of **SAVING ONESELF** for the child.

After swimming to the edge, encourage the child to hold the edge by itself and encourage it to leave the water, supporting the child from behind all the time.

Leg Kicking By The Edge

We lay the child on its stomach at the edge of the pool and swing its legs. We encourage the child to kick its legs by itself.

Sitting On The Edge And Swinging The Legs

This exercise is for children sitting on the edge independently, because we must always have free hands. The child may swing its legs independently, or we may help.

Conclusion

What may one say at the end of a book about swimming and more importantly games for children in water.

First of all, it is difficult to imagine time better spent than during a joint visit of a parent and a child to the swimming pool. Thanks to these visits our child develops well physically and psychologically, an important emotional link is built between us and furthermore, we really enjoy ourselves together. The aim of our book is to encourage you to do this and to discover for yourselves that it is indeed such a good time.

Credits

Photos:	Andrzej Peszek
Chapter Graphic:	©Hemera/Thinkstock
Graphic Bubbles:	©Hemera/Thinkstock
Graphic Figures:	©iStock/Thinkstock
Cover photos:	Andrzej Peszek
Cover Design:	Sabine Groten
Layout:	Cornelia Knorr
Typesetting:	Andreas Reuel
Copy editing:	Sebastian Meyer

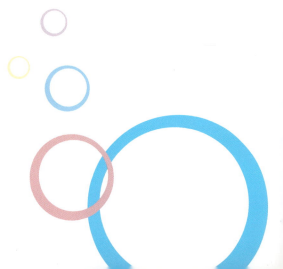